Let Me Use You

Let Me Use You

POETIC BIBLE TRUTHS ABOUT THE FUTURE

↢↣

ERIC ZACK

RESOURCE *Publications* · Eugene, Oregon

LET ME USE YOU
Poetic Bible Truths about the Future

Resource Publications
An Imprint of Wipf and Stock Publishers
199 W. 8th Ave., Suite 3
Eugene, OR 97401

www.wipfandstock.com

PAPERBACK ISBN: 979-8-3852-3358-8
HARDCOVER ISBN: 979-8-3852-3359-5
EBOOK ISBN: 979-8-3852-3360-1

11/25/24

Contents

Rapture

Heaven

The End of Times

Preface

Welcome to my private collection of Christian poetry spanning five total volumes and 173 original, unique poems that I have written over the past thirty years of my life. Each volume deals with key aspects of Christianity and Holy Bible truths that have been revealed to me during my personal struggles. I have organized each one of these into an easy-to-read-and-follow format. Certain lines and stanzas in each of these poems will also have specific Bible verses referenced if you prefer to investigate further, meditate, or dive deeper into the Word.

Volume 1 focuses on God, the Bible, and surrendering. Volume 2 describes Jesus Christ and the need to be born again. Volume 3 highlights important Christian tenants that support living life to its fullest, such as grace, faith, choice, prayer, life, and blessings. Volume 4 depicts evil such as rebellion, pride, Satan, disease, death, and hell. And finally, volume 5 completes my collection with living for the future by applying Christian beliefs and putting this lifestyle into practice in serving others. It covers topics such as the Church, correction, redemption, finding purpose, the rapture, heaven, and the end of times.

I have generally written these poems whenever I had ideas or inspirations come to me and when I had the time to process them, sit down, and compose them (preferably in an uninterrupted manner). Although their actual chronological order has been lost, I feel that there is great benefit in how these poems have been organized for your understanding and reading pleasure. My brain seems to work in this manner by compartmentalizing related topics together. My intention was to document many of my own personal experiences along with my spiritual growth journey, not that I am anyone special in that respect. I'm just an ordinary person whose life experiences have opened my eyes to Jesus at an early point in my young adult life due to certain circumstances. I am so grateful for what has happened in my life and that I was chosen worthy by Jesus to suffer through extreme emotional pain. This has directly led me towards Him. My mom's death was absolutely the worst thing that has ever happened to me; yet in retrospect, it was absolutely the best thing that has ever happened to me. This stark dichotomy remains quite perplexing to me. But I have always wanted to learn what the truth is.

My typical poetry style is to tell an impactful story with powerful emotional details that describe a specific defined topic; and most of them possess some rhythm and rhyming pattern based on the melodies of contemporary music. My hope is that they inspire and speak to you and specifically the younger generation—who might appreciate this form of expression. Most of my poems have been adapted as such, changing the lyrics of these songs to reveal important Bible truths. These melodies are also referenced next to my poem titles. But all of these poems are stand-alone, in that without the melody, they should still make perfect sense. Most of my poems are nonfictional (based on real-life experiences as either being autobiographical or biographical in context); while some are completely fictional (made-up to highlight a particular truth). None of these types really matter in order to highlight the main theme of each poem, nor have these been revealed. One secret I have learned over the years about growing closer to Christ is found in Rom 10:17: "So then faith *comes* by hearing, and hearing by the word of God" (NKJV, italics original). This can be accomplished in many ways and whichever ways you choose; these are pleasing to Him.

I considered my life pretty normal growing up until my mom's death. Then seemingly overnight, my world fell apart, and I felt lost and confused. I didn't know what was happening to me. I asked typical questions like, Why me? and, Why now?, but nothing was revealed to me. Shortly thereafter, my stepfather struggled with alcoholism as a way to self-medicate and numb the emotional pain that he was feeling. And the four of us kids were left to fend for ourselves for our own survival.

I returned to college but barely passed the remaining semesters of my first degree. Nothing as serious as this has ever occurred to me before or ever since thankfully. I was surviving one day at a time and learning valuable lessons as I went through the grieving process internally and privately. It was a slow process for me, as I was still learning who I was, developing into who I wanted to become, all while being a young teenager at heart. All of a sudden, I had to grow up and do so really fast . . . and on my own. Poetry was the only thing that worked for me. Back then, no one had cell phones, and the internet was just created a few years prior to this. Moreover, all of my childhood friends were back in my hometown or away at another college. None of my new college acquaintances could understand what I was going through. Indeed, I felt all alone. Poetry was my only outlet. Putting my emotions down on paper seemed to give these abstract things actual weight, relevance, and true acknowledgment. It also allowed me to literally (physically) and figuratively (emotionally) store my emotions away—as if to feel them, deal with them, learn from them, and then move on from them.

My original intention was simply to try to heal myself—deep down knowing that if I continued to bottle up these emotions over time, I would eventually explode just like a boiling pot of water in a kettle on the stove top. Introverts need time, privacy, and quiet to process difficult experiences. I did not trust anyone enough to share these vulnerabilities with—for fear of judgment, criticism, or simply being dismissed. I never thought my poems would ultimately be worthy of sharing with others to help them in some way. In the midst of tragedy, you can only think of yourself. However, once you pass through that tragedy, you eventually regain a sense of others in the world and can see life and future possibilities and new opportunities more clearly. My hope and prayers are that my poems can help some of you in whatever you are facing today, whether it be serious or trivial, permanent or temporary, or spiritual, psychosocial, and/or physical. I now realize that Jesus was the only one who could heal me and not as a result of my own efforts. My efforts only proved to be futile attempts to try to do what only God can do. I have learned this valuable lesson to let go of certain things that I cannot control.

I have continued writing poetry on a regular basis about life's many experiences, topics, and questions. It has become and remains to be a strong coping mechanism for me when dealing with "life." I have continued to develop and refine my writing abilities and have strengthened my art by adding, practicing, and improving on many tools in my toolbox, so to speak. Sharing these Christian poems has become my priority given today's troubling times with so many broken and lost people. Jesus is the answer to all of your questions!

Introduction

Welcome to the fifth and final volume of my Christian poetry collection. It is entitled *Let Me Use You*, as God's desire to help you and guide your life's work. This collection looks forward to the future and specifically correction, redemption, purpose, the Rapture, heaven, and the end of times.

The first section in this book begins with correction. As a child growing up, I recall being corrected when I did something wrong or potentially dangerous like crossing the street without looking. As a parent myself later in life, I chose to correct my children in the same manner. The Holy Bible describes in Prov 3:12: "For whom the Lord loves He corrects" (AMPC). All of us have been corrected at some point in our lives for many different things, probably multiple times before we fully understood the reasoning behind it. But ultimately, we were corrected because of love. The opposite of this is also true.

The second section describes redemption. Sin is defined by God Himself in the Ten Commandments and then later expanded and detailed by Jesus Christ (Matt 5:28 and 1 John 3:15). After we sin or when we do wrong, God redeems His children. He offered His Son, Jesus Christ, to take our place in death. According to Rom 6:23, "the wages of sin is death" (NIV). But belief in Jesus as your Savior allows God to justly and righteously redeem you to His Son's sinless status and eternal position.

The third section depicts purpose. This section deals with allowing God to use each of us for His specific will and purpose during our brief lives to serve others. When you begin to learn what your spiritual gifts are and eventually find what you have been called to do, all that's left is to surrender your life to do His will. Allow Jesus to work through you every day in every circumstance. "For whoever wants to save their life will lose it, but whoever loses their life for me will save it" (Luke 9:24 NIV). Jesus is talking about how we choose to live in our human body on earth during our lifetime compared to our spirit seeking eternal life.

The fourth section deals with the Rapture. This is the great hope of all Christian—the instantaneous snatching away of believers from this life to receive our new eternal body and to be in the presence of Christ Jesus Himself forevermore (John 14:3; Mark 13:32; Rev 3:10; 1 Cor 15:51-53; and 1 Thess 4:16-18).

The fifth section highlights heaven. The Holy Bible describes three levels of heaven. The third heaven is the current residence of God Himself. However, this third heaven will eventually come down and exist on this planet (Rev 21:1-27). We pray for this in the Lord's Prayer, "Your kingdom come, your will be done, on earth as it is in heaven" (Matt 6:10 NIV). No human knows exactly what heaven will be like, but the Holy Bible gives us some clues. And we know that Jesus Christ is currently seated at the right hand of God (Ps 110:1; 1 Pet 3:22).

The final section focuses on the end of times. I believe that we are very near to the end of times as it is described in the Holy Bible (Matt 24). These Bible verses describe the end of times and includes the signs of Christ's return, perilous times, some details of His glorious return, the parable of the fig tree, and that we need to be ready for His coming. Further, the dangers of the last days are described in 2 Tim 3: 1-5, specifically common things that we observe today. But as stated in Luke 21:28, "Now when these things begin to occur, stand tall and lift up your heads [in joy], because [suffering ends as] your redemption is drawing near" (AMP, brackets original).

Thank you and may God bless you. Please enjoy!

CORRECTION

Savior

(Adapted from the melody of "Halo" by Beyonce)

As selfishness stains my heart	1 Cor 10:24
I'm upset not getting my way	
I only care about myself	
Your ways are no longer my ways	Isa 55:8
I strayed away from You; depart	
Not knowing how far I fell	
I finally see Your light shining	John 8:12
I desire it to bode well	

It's like I'm standing naked	Heb 4:13
I'm embarrassed by this hatred	
You, I've desecrated	
I'm not gonna let this go on	

I thought I was a good Christian	
But I've proven myself to fail	Eph 2:10–13
Truly Jesus, You're my Savior	1 John 4:14
You're the only way that I'll prevail	
I'm not the person I was before	2 Cor 5:17
I surrender my life to You	Luke 9:23–24
Truly Jesus, You're my Savior	
Won't you please help me improve?	

You're my Savior, Savior, Savior, Savior
You're my Savior, Savior, Savior, Savior

I denied making these mistakes
I've hurt those who're closest to me
I rejected their uniqueness
And expect them to think like me

I swore that I'd denounce them
If their choices they continued to defend
I couldn't have been more wrong
I hope our relationships will eventually mend

It's like I'm standing naked
I'm embarrassed by this hatred
You, I've desecrated
I'm not gonna let this go on

I thought I was a good Christian
But I've proven myself to fail
Truly Jesus, You're my Savior
You're the only way that I'll prevail
I'm not the person I was before
I surrender my life to You
Truly Jesus, You're my Savior
Won't you please help me improve?

You're my Savior, Savior, Savior
You're my Savior, Savior, Savior
You're my Savior, Savior, Savior
Savior, oh; Savior, oh

I thought I was a good Christian
But I've proven myself to fail
Truly Jesus, You're my Savior
You're the only way that I'll prevail
I'm not the person I was before
I surrender my life to You
Truly Jesus, You're my Savior
Won't you please help me improve?

You're my Savior, Savior, Savior
You're my Savior, Savior, Savior
You're my Savior, Savior, Savior
Savior, oh; Savior, oh

Possess

(Adapted from the melody of "COMPLETE MESS" by 5 Seconds of Summer)

I'm a student of Your Word, but fail to act	
I'm ashamed	Matt 7:17–20
I'm the only one to blame, rabbi	

I receive Your grace	
While on the cross, Jesus took my place	1 Cor 15:3–8
How did I ever deserve this exchange, thereby?	

All my errors and past mistakes	
You willingly have erased	Matt 12:31–32
In preparation to rule after this life	2 Tim 2:11–13

Oh, You convict me indeed	John 16:7–11
You convict me indeed	
You convict me indeed—possess	

If you truly love me	
My commandments you'll obey	John 14:15–31
That you may prosper in all things and glorify	3 John 1:2

Jesus as my LORD and Savior	
His sacrifice foretold	Heb 10:10
As He is today; in this world, so am I	1 John 4:17

Even though I'm an imperfect creation and eventually will betray	
I am still a part of Your Church, Your bride	Eph 5:22–33

Oh, You convict me indeed
You convict me indeed
You convict me indeed—possess

Oh, You convict me indeed
You convict me indeed
You convict me indeed—possess

I'm a student of Your Word, but fail to act—I'm ashamed
I'm the only one to blame, rabbi

Oh, You convict me indeed
You convict me indeed
You convict me indeed—possess

Oh, You convict me indeed
You convict me indeed
You convict me indeed—possess

REDEMPTION

God's Steward

(Adapted from the melody of "Woman" by Doja Cat)

God's steward, God's steward, God's steward	Matt 25:14–30
Let me be Your steward; steward, steward, steward	
I can be Your steward; steward, steward, steward	

Heard Your pleas?	Matt 26:36–56
But God chose to ignore, and He made You bleed	Rom 5:9
You then died, but resurrected indeed	Luke 9:22
And now Your name saves and forgives	
It exceeds everything—agreed	Heb 9:15–22

You can designate	
An unselfish advocate	John 14:16
Make all things orchestrate	Eph 1:11
And be God's intermediate	

The Law, the stone replaced with grace	Rom 6:14
Our former damnation erased	Rom 6:23
Righteousness and peace will embrace	Ps 145:18
God, let me be Your steward	

Let me be Your steward; steward, steward, steward
I can be your steward; steward, steward, steward
Let me be Your steward; steward, steward, steward
I can be your steward; steward, steward, steward

You get what you deserve, that's karma	
But you reap what you sow is now a farmer	Gal 6:7–9
With grace and mercy, Jesus took us farther	2 John 1:3
His righteousness for our sins, he bartered	1 Cor 1:30

In our lives, He wants to be predominant	Col 1:18
He cares about all our cares, cognizant	1 Pet 5:7
You and I in the highest court, He acquits	Rom 3:22–24
The ultimate sacrifice without blemish He fits	1 Pet 1:18–21

We're no longer in debt	
No more sadness, no regret	Rev 21:4
He remembers our sins no more, forgets	Heb 8:12
All of our trespasses are offset	Matt 6:14–15

This was always God's plan to redeem	John 10:18
This is the Bible's fundamental theme	
Salvation through the shedding of His bloodstream	Heb 9:11–22
Poured onto the mercy seat	
Of the Ark of the Covenant	Exod 25:17
Protected by the cherubim	Ezek 10:20–22
Before the rapture is God's final generation	1 Thess 4
Known as the Benjamin	Deut 33:12

Five times more blessings than its predecessor	Eph 4:11–16
Significantly taken altogether	
Call upon the name of the LORD whosoever	Rom 10:13
The ultimate specimen, the perfect medicine	
Steward	

Let me be Your steward; steward, steward, steward
I can be your steward; steward, steward, steward
Let me be Your steward; steward, steward, steward
I can be your steward; steward, steward, steward

Feed My Lambs

(Adapted from the melody of "Team" by Lorde)

I know my new purpose
It was quietly revealed on the TV
It became clear like a bright day
It makes perfect sense that He'll provide the way . . .

After Jesus' death   John 21:1
He appeared once again
The disciples went fishing   John 21:3
But they caught nothing that night   John 21:5
Then Jesus said to them
"Throw your net on the right side"   John 21:6[1]
They were unable to haul in the load of net-breaking fish

John and Peter recognized the LORD
It truly was indeed the LORD
Then Peter quickly jumped into the water towards
    Him   John 21:–7

Peter was redeemed, He was forgiven and restored
to his former stature, continue what he was to do
And then Jesus said feed my lambs, take care of
    my sheep   John 21:15–16
And then He said feed my sheep and follow me   John 21:17–19

Although Peter betrayed Jesus three times before
    His crucifixion—conviction   Luke 22:54–62
Jesus wanted Peter to know for certain that love
    doesn't originate with him   1 John 4:19
But that God's eternal love is possible because of Christ   Rom 3:24
'Cause if you believe, you can receive   Matt 21:22

---

1. NIV.

Peter was redeemed, He was forgiven and restored
to his former stature, continue what he was to do
And then Jesus said, "Feed my lambs," "Take care of my sheep"
And then He said, "Feed my sheep" and "Follow me"

I'm teaching nursing students the science and art
    to become aware—prepare
I'm serving people with cancer who need physical
    and emotional care—repair

Peter was redeemed, He was forgiven and restored
to his former stature, continue what he was to do
And then Jesus said, "Feed my lambs," "Take care of my sheep"
And then He said, "Feed my sheep" and "Follow me"

Please minister My Word   Acts 20:24
Now you know, please minister My Word
Please minister My Word
Now you know, now you know, now you know

PURPOSE

Mom, You'd Be Proud

(Adapted from the melody of "The Child in Us" by Enigma)

Today is the birth of my dream
Conceived long ago as it may seem
No longer can I roam on the path to flee
But rather I shall walk on the path that I lead

I answer your call, I answer your plea
To follow in your shoes, to live by your creed
No more do I sleep lazily beneath the tree
But rather I strive planting forth your sacred seed

You heard me clear, you heard me loud
And surely Mom, you'd be proud . . .

I open my heart so that others can feed
I expose my soul, I live and breathe
I collapse from these efforts, I am prone to fatigue
I am hurt and I cry; I suffer, and I bleed

But soon I accept this role of your plead
I'm told there's no escape, and I cannot scream
Your duty is now mine, and my future is foreseen
I'm here to love the sick, I'm here to meet their needs

1 John 3:17

You heard me clear, you heard me loud
And surely Mom, you'd be proud . . .

Your expectations for me are difficult indeed
The unselfish person that you want me to be   Luke 6:35–36
Dedicated to the ones fighting cancer in their dreams
Inspired by your life, driven by the world's intrigue

LET ME USE YOU

And if you could see all the things I've achieved
Just to take a minute to look deep inside of me
Then happily you'd find the core of my good deeds
With all the remnants of death and your past that I've freed

You heard me clear, you heard me loud
And surely Mom, you'd be proud . . .

For Their Sake

(Adapted from the melody of "Up Against It" by Pet Shop Boys)

At sundown, sighing, we dry our tears
From friends and those who're no longer here
We use their souls to guide us forward
We smile in their eyes

MOTIVATION
They must have appeared just to help us revere
Our INSPIRATION
They must have returned to share what they've learned

At nightfall, wishing, we held His staff   Gal 2:20
For those of whom we've crossed their paths
We request the amnesty they deserve
They smile at our appeal

INCLINATION
We do what we teach so that they we can reach   Matt 23:1–3
Our MATURATION
This comes with the seed to defend those in need

At nighttime, kneeling, we're by our bed   Eph 3:14
With God watching above our heads
We share with Him our thoughts unspoken
He smiles as we pray

His SALVATION
He shows us the light buried deep in the night   John 8:12
Our DESTINATION
We walk down the road that He has bestowed

In darkness, walking, our eyes consume
The souls floating about our room
Their echoing voices serenade us
They smile as they fly

FASCINATION
They're here to explain why we must remain
Our OBLIGATION
For those faced with fate, we exist for their sake

His Voice Calling

I always hated God for making my life what it was
So much that I'd close my ears to His voice calling
Never would I accept His ways
only because he made me wear the shoes that I have worn
And after learning a lesson from a movie, of all things
I saw what I haven't seen . . .
That there is a purpose to everything   Prov 16:4
And that there are many lessons to be learned
It is life, and yes, it is death
but it is what you make it to be

Learning to accept death, learning to accept life . . .
Now, it makes a lot of sense
Who I am, what I'm here for
And why I will sacrifice for others   Luke 9:24
So, at this time in my life, while I think alone in my room
Yet in His presence
Suddenly, I see Reason . . . I see Destiny;
I see . . . whatever I make it to be

The Light at the End of the Tunnel

Death has certainly stained my soul
I can't remember my life before
No more joy facing strife
Feeling pain and numb to life
I seem to be stuck in survival mode

I can't break free, I can't move on
Not really sure what lies beyond
I toss and turn, I cannot sleep
My chest is tight, I cannot breathe
Who really knows just how I'll respond?

Today, my dreams resemble terror
Not sure how much more I can bear
Can't believe this is my norm
My spirit cries to be reborn   John 3:5–7
My face is forever marked with despair

I used to be different, I used to smile
When will I forget about all these trials?
Dark clouds cover. Can I recover?
Will there be another? What'll I discover?
Or shall I dwell in the past, stuck in denial?

I look for the good, I look for the light
I look deep inside myself and keep praying despite
My nerves break down, the hurt makes me frown
Then the only sound is my heart as it pounds
My being's bruised, but it soon shines bright

Indeed, these experiences are quite tough
When will really enough be enough?
They do scare me; they're not ordinary
They're disciplinary, but necessary
To mold me into what He wants me to become   Isa 64:8

What is the meaning? What should I learn?
How can I help others with their struggles in turn?
No time for tears, lay down my fears   1 Pet 3:6
I can't disappear, I must persevere
I won't look back; alas, there's no return

I'll share my pain, I'll share my story
Lift them up, up towards Your glory
Face to face, share Your grace
A long embrace for the human race
Helping them escape their earthly purgatory   John 14:6

Search and Rescue

(Adapted from the melody of "Lover" by Taylor Swift)

Many Christians believe they're on a cruise vacation
They enjoy all the food, they choose their fun
They're looking forward to heaven as their final destination
But they don't realize that their journey's just begun

We follow where He goes   Luke 18:22
And we're looking out below—wherever, whomever
We're all situated in a paddle boat
We're actually on a search and rescue   Matt 28:19–20

Many of us seek to secure our own salvation
This is our life, it's that simple
Our goal is to do what it takes to avoid damnation
Not realizing that just loving God's not enough   2 Cor 12:9–10

We follow where He goes
And we're looking out below—wherever, whomever
We're all situated in a paddle boat (whenever, however)
We're actually on a search and rescue

We're all called to help save our fellow man   Rom 6:6
With the help of Christ Jesus seated at His right hand   1 Pet 3:22
Allowing Him to use us as vessels of His will   Eph 3:20
His crew

Life presents difficulties brought upon you   John 16:33
To surrender to Him and feel the breakthrough   Matt 11:28
Despite the darkness, He'll help you pass through   Ps 23:4
Always there, renewed   2 Cor 4:16

And He'll ensure that your life will be complete
Taking your place at the cross will be your receipt   1 Pet 3:18
Rescued

We follow where He goes
And we're looking out below—wherever, whomever
We're all situated in a paddle boat (whenever, however)

We're actually on a search and rescue
We're actually on a search and rescue
We're actually on a search and rescue
We're actually on a search and rescue mission

Forgive

(Adapted from the melody of "You Get What You Give"
by New Radicals)

If you love God, you will want to appease	Matt 7:21
Make it routine, since He reigns supreme	
By His grace, you live; won't you agree?	Rom 10:9–10
Penalties coming your way—it depends	
With what else to others that you extend,	
What we've done, and our motivations like why	Luke 6:45
So, when you come a-calling	
Do not approach Him with fright (fright)	Isa 41:10
But rather a sense of belonging, delight	Isa 43:1
Jesus reconciled you: don't lay low	2 Cor 5:18
Jesus reconciled you: don't be stressed	
Our bodies and minds are renewed	Rom 12:1–2
Don't erupt; as an alternative—give	
Don't reject, forgive 'cause Jesus forgives	Eph 4:32

Watch what you dole out, your response, or suffer without

Overwhelmed? Don't just proceed to hostile	
Fear revoke, incorporate love into your lifestyle	John 13:34
Find your niche; trust me, it'll be worth your while	
So, when you come a-calling	
Forgiveness is recommended . . . to others	
Instead of just forsaking, amen	Heb 10:25

Jesus reconciled you: don't lay low
Jesus reconciled you: don't be stressed
Our bodies and minds are renewed
Don't erupt; as an alternative—give
Don't reject, forgive 'cause Jesus forgives

The LORD gives all of us a fresh start
Confess your sins to one another   Jas 5:16
Your words have weight
Remain aligned through His bloodline   1 John 1:7

Jesus reconciled you: don't lay low
Jesus reconciled you: don't be stressed
Our bodies and minds are renewed
Don't erupt; as an alternative—give
Don't reject, forgive 'cause Jesus forgives
Don't lay low, Jesus reconciled you: overflow

Magnify, satisfy, reveal, and sacrifice
Forgive 'cause Jesus forgives

You've been pardoned, mercy finding   Eph 1:3–10
Every day, Christ's likeness striving   2 Cor 3:18
Facing hardships while your smiling
Serving others is awe-inspiring
Forgive seventy times seven   Matt 18:21–22
Especially if you want to get into heaven
We make mistakes, watch your reactions
Turn around, or He'll abandon   Matt 3:2

Don't lay low, don't be stressed
Don't erupt, don't reject
Overflow

Be the World's Light

(Adapted from the melody of "Last Friday Night (T.G.I.F.)" by Katy Perry)

I have this thought in which I dread that I'm mistaken for the dead
I hope one day to be exhumed, quickly released from this tomb
Freed from this deep reservoir; this is my greatest fear by far
I climb out, then the ground crew claimed that this was voodoo

Our bodies are finite, try to be polite and renewed; excel
Be kind and sincere, selfless, and mature; so, you prove His lamp

Be the world's light   Matt 5:14
Shine bright as the sun drops, put down your laptop
Share love in your response; be the world's light
Poor attitudes disregard, be patient when stress bombards
Don't track the scorecard; be the world's light

Be careful of your remarks, respect His hierarch   Isa 46:9–10
Don't leave a question mark; be the world's light
You're no longer under Law because God's your father-in-law
    and then some   Rom 6:14

Be the world's light, you're born again
Be the world's light, you're born again

No need to take any shots, you're surrounded by glass and rocks
Know what you stand for, high expectations even more
Seek the Spirit, but I digress; possess, not just profess   1 Cor 3:21
Always be of full avail; continue until you prevail   2 Tim 4:7

Our bodies are finite, try to be polite and renewed; excel
Be kind and sincere, selfless, and mature; so, you prove His lamp

Be the world's light
Shine bright as the sun drops, put down your laptop
Share love in your response; be the world's light
Poor attitudes disregard, be patient when stress bombards
Don't track the scorecard; be the world's light

Be careful of your remarks, respect His hierarch
Don't leave a question mark; be the world's light
You're no longer under Law because God's your father-in-law
    and then some

Be the world's light, you're born again
Be the world's light, you're born again
Be the world's light, be the world's light

Shine bright as the sun drops, put down your laptop
Share love in your response; be the world's light
Poor attitudes disregard, be patient when stress bombards
Don't track the scorecard; be the world's light

Be careful of your remarks, respect His hierarch
Don't leave a question mark; be the world's light
You're no longer under Law because God's your father-in-law
    and then some

Be the world's light, you're born again
Be the world's light, you're born again
You're born again

Find Your Calling

(Adapted from the melody of "Being Boring" by Pet Shop Boys)

When you're young, you have so many activities
The sky's the limit and the temp's 80 degrees
Everything's right, there's no reservations
With so much delight, and no such worries
You're stress free from all of these

Too much fun and experimentation in
The bright sun, then the day's done
Go to bed and look up towards
The ceiling; your concerns are not the Lord's   Phil 2:21

It takes time to find your calling   Eph 4:1–6
We have no awareness of this other realm
It takes time to find your calling
Learning what your talk and walk represent
To become someone who in fact greatly impacts
By serving others that connects   Gal 6:10

It begins with deep meditation
Followed by action in getting educated
And if you want to be successful
It's instrumental to become prayerful   Ps 4:1
With the gift of longevity   Ps 91:16

We are warned not to be conformed   Rom 12:2
But rather transformed from this world
Renewing your spirit's its own reward
Seeking Christ's wisdom for what's in store   Eph 1:17

It takes time to find your calling
We have no awareness of this other realm
It takes time to find your calling
Learning what your talk and walk represent
To become someone who in fact greatly impacts
By serving others that connects
Your expectations will be surpassed, your life's been mapped
He will provide you with direction

And you'll go through different stages
Growing from mistakes and situations
Let it be known that God's forgiving   Col 1:14
Ask with supplication and thanksgiving   Phil 4:6
He will hear all of your pleas   1 John 5:15
I'm so grateful that I have already seen
The impact of some of my childhood dreams
Through His grace and new mercies   Heb 4:16
How I've elevated others certainly

It takes time to find your calling
We have no awareness of this other realm
It takes time to find your calling
Learning what your talk and walk represent
To become someone who in fact greatly impacts
By serving others that connects
Your expectations will be surpassed, your life's been mapped
He will provide you with direction

It takes time to find your calling
You're blessed when you've been called
It takes time to find your calling
You're blessed when you've been called

This World

(Adapted from the melody of "Sad Robot World" by Pet Shop Boys)

Though we're in this world	2 Cor 10:3–13
There'll be another chapter	
A more important matter	
You're not of this world	John 18:36
We have a special mission	
With worthier ambitions	
It will be revealed someday	Isa 2:12
Most will face condemnation	
An unimaginable doomsday	
But there's a path to salvation	Rom 10:9
Though we're in this world	
It requires an admission	
Just one heart-felt petition	Rom 10:9–11
You're not of this world	
The goal's to receive deliverance	
To fail is due to ignorance	
There's the truth, the life, the way	John 14:6
Jesus is the standard	
Surely, He'll receive you today	
He's reaching openhanded	Ps 145:10–18
Though we're in this world	
Soon, we'll be together	
With indescribable treasures	Matt 6:20
You're not of this world	
Continue testifying	John 15:27
Inspiring and edifying	Eph 4:29–32

Persecution for Christ

(Adapted from the melody of "hot girl bummer" by blackbear)

Fiery trials will be sent towards you   1 Pet 4:12–13
The world hates Christians, and they hate me too
Be faithful until death ensues   Rev 2:10

God has promised not to abandon   Deut 31:6–8
He is present; your companion
His desire, it's His passion
To grow the Church through soul expansion   Matt 28:19

Sheep surrounded by wolves attacks   Matt 7:15
To see precisely what's your reaction
They'll be purposeful to pick fights
Hoping, waiting to see what ignites

Testing will bombard you
But you're blessed sharing suffering with Christ   Phil 3:10

They'll argue all things disputed   John 16:33
Up in your face and hope you're muted
Turning your kindness around, exploiting
But their understanding's so convoluted

When insulted, remain stable
Know that you are securely rooted
Today, a hundred-fold rewarded   Matt 19:29
For God's sake when you're persecuted

Fiery trials will be sent towards you
The world hates Christians, and they hate me too
Be faithful until death ensues
It's their source of satisfaction
To hide their eternal destination

Fiery trials will be sent towards you
The world hates Christians, and they hate me too
Fiery trials will be sent towards you
Until the time of your extraction
When you enter into heaven's mansion

God's power is made perfect in weakness	2 Cor 12:9
Simple innocence to bear witness	Rom 8:16
Stand, hold firm, and show devotion	1 Pet 5:12
To God's standards for a promotion	Jas 4:10

Ignorance or negligence, it's sad
Driven by emotion
What's exactly in the Bible
This is what God's revealed; this is what He has spoken

They'll argue all things disputed
Up in your face and hope you're muted
Turning your kindness around, exploiting
But their understanding's so convoluted

The Lord will rescue you, so be enabled	
Don't compromise, never diluted	
Today, a hundred-fold rewarded	
For God's sake when you're persecuted	Matt 5:10–12

Fiery trials will be sent towards you
The world hates Christians, and they hate me too
Be faithful until death ensues
A servant's not greater than his master
Sharing the truth is a form of compassion

Fiery trials will be sent towards you
The world hates Christians, and they hate me too
Fiery trials will be sent towards you
Without your salt and light, imagine
The impact to this world, what would happen

They'll argue all things disputed
Up in your face and hope you're muted
Turning your kindness around, exploiting
But their understanding's so convoluted

They'll argue all things disputed
Up in your face and hope you're muted
Turning your kindness around, exploiting
But their understanding's so convoluted

In conclusion, in conclusion, in . . .
And you want Christians to be restrained? Never!

Fiery trials will be sent towards you
The world hates Christians, and they hate me too
Be faithful until death ensues
Because of Christ's grace transaction
The hurt of the second death's been retracted
Fiery trials will be sent towards you

The world hates Christians, and they hate me too
Fiery trials will be sent towards you
Don't resign or yield to inaction
Satan will continue as the assassin

RAPTURE

The Rapture

(Adapted from the melody of "So Cold" by Mahalo & DLMT, feat. Lily Denning)

I look through the clouds towards a bright	1 Thess 4:17
Light being pulled up to check it out	
Fast forward and faster than the speed of light	
Not possible, body without	

'Cause it's so far from what we know
It's so far from what we know

'Cause when we leave our dead bodies	Phil 3:21
Behind, long gone; we're now on our way	
Up through the atmosphere, up	2 Cor 12:2–4

Sense of freedom, never encountered
Weightlessness made up
Reality unfolds, unfolds, unfolds, unfolds

And we're now young again in an instant	Job 33:25
Moment not questioning the reason no doubt	
Enjoying paradise with Jesus	Luke 23:43
In His mansion next to the streets of gold throughout	John 14:2
Heaven unfolds, heaven unfolds	

And I can sing with angels or among the saints that worship	Ps 138:1
So, I can be with Christ	2 Cor 5:8
And I rule with Jesus as His elect in the last days	Rev 20:6
Receive His sacrifice	Rom 3:25

'Cause it's so far from what we know
It's so far from what we know

'Cause when we are given new bodies	2 Cor 5:1–10
To house our spirits	
And our souls distinct	
We are Christ's new creatures	2 Cor 5:17

The old portions are now passed away	Rom 6:6–7
Behold, new things have come	
And so; heaven unfolds, unfolds, unfolds, unfolds	

We Don't Know When

(Adapted from the melody of "Monsters" by All Time Low, feat. Demi Lovato & blackbear)

Don't forget oil to burn in your lights
Or you may miss the groom and his bride   Matt 25:1
Don't be distracted or occupied or you may be left outside

Don't want to show up late or fall asleep as well   Matt 25:2
Don't be caught off-guard or turned away—what a bombshell
Procrastination is so revealing, wouldn't you agree with me?
Don't miss out on the drinking and the eating
All alone in summary

I'm discovering—don't forget oil to burn in your lights   Matt 25:4
Or you may miss the groom and his bride
Don't be distracted or occupied or you may be left outside

Why would you be foolish and risk being denied?
Why do you set yourself up to be chastised?
Why not plan? Why improvise and be cast out in surprise?

Our gathering unto Him in a twinkling of an eye   1 Cor 15:52
The Day of Christ is at hand, so don't consider
          even blinking   Phil 1:6
If you aren't ready, then certainly you are risking
Being stuck in this world, and likely you are sinking

Be careful not to agonize, don't miss out on what awaits
Don't be caught with your pants down, really just in case
Be ready and prepared, and instead be at peace   Matt 24:44
For the Great Tribulation you'll be spared   Matt 24:21

I'm discovering—don't forget oil to burn in your lights
Or you may miss the groom and his bride
Don't be distracted or occupied or you may be left outside

Why would you be foolish and risk being denied?
Why do you set yourself up to be chastised?
Why not plan? Why improvise and be cast out in surprise?

Consider yourself warned, just like it's said
Don't be stupid, don't be misled
Don't be distracted or occupied or you may be left outside

Dread, facing the forthcoming mass bloodshed
This is the truth, so go ahead
Don't be distracted or occupied or you may be left outside

I'm discovering—don't forget oil to burn in your lights
Or you may miss the groom and his bride
Don't be distracted or occupied or you may be left outside

Why would you be foolish and risk being denied?
Why do you set yourself up to be chastised?
Why not plan? Why improvise and be cast out in surprise?

Occupied? Or you may be left outside

In a Twinkling of an Eye

(Adapted from the melody of "When You're Gone" by Shawn Mendes)

The end of the world's coming—dammit	
The end is prophesied full of fire, whereas	Matt 24:21

If you seek Jesus, if you pursue	
Then you might be spared and might be withdrew	Matt 6:33

We're moving fast head-on
Head-on

The tribulation will precede Armageddon	Rev 16:16
You want to be foregone	
The tribulation will certainly precede Armageddon	

You don't want the apocalypse
A solar eclipse, a total eclipse
You don't want to leave it to chance that you're still here on earth
    considering
We're moving fast head-on

You want an early exit rendezvous	1 Thess 4:17
Trust me, you don't want to stay for the barbecue	
You want to avoid the judicial review	Rev 20:11–13
You can look forward to a switcheroo	

We're moving fast head-on
Head-on

The tribulation will precede Armageddon
You want to be foregone
The tribulation will certainly precede Armageddon

You don't want the apocalypse
A solar eclipse, a total eclipse
You don't want to leave it to chance that you're still here
    on earth considering
We're moving fast head-on

The world was created in just six days   Exod 20:11
And yet God's sixth day is about to play
No more appeals, it's time for those to repay

We're moving fast head-on

The world was created in just six days
And yet God's sixth day is about to play
No more appeals, it's time for those to repay

We're moving fast head-on
Head-on

The tribulation will precede Armageddon
You want to be foregone
The tribulation will certainly precede Armageddon

You don't want the apocalypse
A solar eclipse, a total eclipse
You don't want to leave it to chance that you're still here
    on earth considering
We're moving fast head-on

HEAVEN

Heaven Above

(Adapted from the melody of "Show Me Love" by Robin S.)

Ah, yeah, yeah, yeah, yeah
There's a heaven above   Ps 113:4

There's an entire realm that's located high up in the air
It's hidden from our view
But it's there Jesus declares, declares   Deut 10:14

This is a very special place where there are
    no more tears   Rev 21:4
No mourning or crying; pain and death both disappear

The gates are brilliant like pearls, so beautiful and grand
And the streets are all lined with gold; it's our real-life homeland

Don't mistake this for a dream, there's a heaven above
Paradise is being in God's presence
There's a heaven above   Luke 23:43

If you believe in Jesus, if He's your LORD and Savior   Acts 16:31
Then you're an heir and He'll return to you
A place has been prepared   John 14:3

You're a child of God preserved
You get what you don't deserve   Rom 8:17
Entry into heaven through His grace, forgiveness,
    and salvation conferred   Eph 2:8

And Jesus said to the weary, "Come unto Me"   Matt 11:28
Indeed, "I will give you rest"
"My burden is light; my yoke is easy"   Matt 11:30

Don't mistake this for a dream, there's a heaven above
Paradise is being in God's presence; there's a heaven above

"Know Me, know Me"; you must   Matt 7:23
You can't dismiss the possibility
You don't want the alternative
To be lonely; "As I am love"   1 John 4:16

Surely, surely, surely, you can be saved   Eph 2:8
I'll approach you individually
I offer joy, I offer you My grace   Eph 2:7
I'll take you to the Promised Land

Jesus' return is near   Matt 24:3–14
Believe and you shall be spared
He will judge all mankind; for some   Heb 9:27
It'll be their worst nightmare, nightmare

The first heaven and earth will pass away   Rev 21:1
And the third heaven will appear   Luke 23:43
The New Jerusalem will descend   Rev 21:2
A new beginning will transcend

Unbelievers will be punished so severely   Rev 20:15
I hope you fully understand
My disciples will be cherished dearly

Don't mistake this for a dream, there's a heaven above
Paradise is being in God's presence; there's a heaven above

Golden City

(Adapted from the melody of "Silver City"
by Ghostland Observatory)

Well, I dream of a golden city
By Your side called to reign   Rev 20:6
Forgetting all that's busy
In this life—what remains?

Well, I dream of a golden city
Placed high up in the clouds   2 Cor 12:2
In reality, not theory
All that's beautiful abounds

Well, I think that you've prepared a room
    in Your mansion   John 14:2
And I think that it bears my name
    as You proclaimed it so   John 14:3

Well, I dream of a golden city
With all things to sustain
In my heart it's revealed clearly
Our paradise regained   Luke 23:43

Well, I'm thankful I choose to enter
    through the narrow door   Luke 13:24
And you should consider doing the same thing for sure

Well, I dream of a golden city
Where all that's good is displayed
It's hard to describe it sincerely For our ticket's been prepaid

Well, I dream of a golden city
Where there's no more decay   Rev 21:4
And you can enter it surely
If "Jesus is my LORD," you say   Mark 16:16

Well, I think that in order for us towards God
    to draw near   Jas 4:8
Jesus said that for "Whoever has ears, let them hear"   Mark 4:9

Well, I dream of a golden city
It's more amazing than it sounds
His light shines so brilliantly   John 8:12
I've tried my best to expound

When Jesus Stands Up

(Adapted from the melody of "The Bones" by Maren Morris)

Although Jesus is seated, sometimes He'll rise   Luke 22:69
When you exceed; what does this imply?

There are only a few conditions when this He chooses
And to His delight, His response to your action is produced

When He receives you, standing—He's flattered
You'll be by His side in His presence thereafter   2 Cor 5:8
Heaven quakes; and then your name Jesus proclaims
Like when you speak truth in any given situation
Possibly martyred in some tribulation   Acts 7:55–56
When you advance the kingdom of God for good
These are the times when Jesus stands up   Acts 7:55–56

Some will be awestruck, but most will question why
Knowing this would interrupt; they're not ready to die
No, most people aren't willing to try to understand this
"Go and make disciples of all nations" and start baptizing
      Matt 28:19[2]

When He receives you, standing—He's flattered
You'll be by His side in His presence thereafter
Heaven quakes; and then your name Jesus proclaims
Like when you speak truth in any given situation
Possibly martyred in some tribulation
When you advance the kingdom of God for good
These are the times when Jesus stands up, when Jesus stands up

---

2. NIV.

He receives you, standing—it's because He's flattered
You'll be by His side in His presence, in His presence thereafter
He receives you, standing—it's because He's flattered
You'll be by His side in His presence, in His presence thereafter

When He receives you, standing—He's flattered
You'll be by His side in His presence thereafter
Heaven quakes; and then your name Jesus proclaims
Like when you speak truth in any given situation
Possibly martyred in some tribulation
When you advance the kingdom of God for good
These are the times when Jesus stands up

THE END OF TIMES

It's All God's Plan

(Adapted from the melody of "Disturbia" by Rihanna)

We're all human, we renege
We've grown so cold-hearted
Look at the way that we live
The true faith we departed
A deeper hole we constantly dig
Descending a path that's uncharted
Our normal has become profane

Do you desire eternal life? I ask you
What will it take for you to see the light? I beg of you
If you reject Jesus Christ, then damn you   1 John 2:22
Want to be triumphant?

Blinded by a bright light and accompanied by thunder
You won't have to think twice, you'll awaken from your slumber
Time to pay the price; a sword out of His mouth
     to slaughter   Rev 19:15
Indeed, His grace is sufficing   2 Cor 12:9

Remember, it's all God's plan   Ps 40:5
Those who are righteous will reunite   Isa 41:10
It's all God's plan
You'll be harshly judged despite
It's all God's plan
There's a penalty for pride   Prov 16:18
It's all God's plan
It's all God's plan

Disobedience since man's fall   Rom 5:12
Interest on our debt incurring
All our lives are in default
There's a plan for transferring   Acts 16:30–33
Imagine our gall
God's holy, He's appalled
Want to be free from judgment?   John 8:11

Do you desire eternal life? I ask you
What will it take for you to see the light? I beg of you
If you reject Jesus Christ, then damn you
Do you want to prosper?

Blinded by a bright light and accompanied by thunder
You won't have to think twice, you'll awaken from your slumber
Time to pay the price; a sword out of His mouth to slaughter
Indeed, His grace is sufficing

Remember, it's all God's plan
Returning like a thief in the night   Rev 16:15
It's all God's plan
If you're guilty, He'll ignite   Rev 20:15
It's all God's plan
He's justified, He is right
It's all God's plan
It's all God's plan

The end is near, and the time is coming   Matt 24:3
Trying to resist society is so troubling   John 15:19
But if you want to know
The Book of Revelation says it so

Blinded by a bright light and accompanied by thunder
You won't have to think twice, you'll awaken from your slumber
Time to pay the price; a sword out of His mouth to slaughter
Indeed, His grace is sufficing

Remember, it's all God's plan
Living in today's world, I don't like
It's all God's plan
Do you side with the antichrist?   1 John 2:22
It's all God's plan
God's in charge, only He can decide   John 13:3
It's all God's plan
It's all God's plan

Your Destruction

(Adapted from the melody of "Unstoppable" by Sia)

With trials, your faith is tested until you're worn down
The end results are blessings abound
This glorifies the divine   Rev 21:7

Oh yeah, oh yeah
Things aren't really as they appear
If you're a believer, there's nothing to fear
This is by His design   Mark 5:36

Yeah, yeah
Hear the words of the LORD, His return won't be
    a lamb   Rev 19:15
Hear the words of the LORD, His return won't be a lamb

Your destruction is nearing as the entire earth quakes   Matt 24:7
This is Biblical as every knee will bow to His name   Rom 14:11

This is allowable because society has decayed   Rom 5:12
Please be cognizant, your destruction will be doomsday

Your destruction is delayed
Your destruction is delayed   Eccl 8:11–13
Your destruction is delayed
Your destruction is delayed

Make a vow, there's no room for you to doubt
Time's running out as judgment mounts
Forget about being proud   1 Sam 2:3

Yeah, yeah
It's so, you're headed for a permanent deathblow
But there is a secret way for you to forego
Believe and declare with your mouth   Rom 10:9

Yeah, yeah
Hear the words of the LORD, His return won't be a lamb
Hear the words of the LORD, His return won't be a lamb

Your destruction is nearing as the entire earth quakes
This is Biblical as every knee will bow to His name

This is allowable because society has decayed
Please be cognizant, your destruction will be doomsday

Your destruction is delayed, your destruction is delayed
Your destruction is delayed, your destruction is delayed

Your destruction is delayed, your destruction is delayed
Your destruction is delayed, your destruction is delayed

You have a countdown; repent or you'll be damned   Matt 24:3
You have a countdown; repent or you'll be damned

Your destruction is nearing as the entire earth quakes
This is Biblical as every knee will bow to His name

This is allowable because society has decayed
Please be cognizant, your destruction will be doomsday

Your destruction is delayed, your destruction is delayed
Your destruction is delayed, your destruction is delayed

Your destruction is delayed, your destruction is delayed
Your destruction is delayed, your destruction is delayed

You Can't Stop My God

(Adapted from the melody of "You Can't Stop the Girl"
by Bebe Rexha)

Oh, many persecute Christians	Matt 10:23
They're all told it's okay to	John 15:18
So, they do—but why?	
And, oh, it's been prophesied though	
Just as Jesus said so	
Indeed, the end is near	Matt 24:3

You can't stop God's plan from happening	
You can't stop the world from panicking	
"The truth will set you free," oh	John 8:31–32
You can't stop His angels from ravaging	
You can't stop this world from vanishing	Matt 24:35
"The truth will set you free," oh	
You can't stop my God	

They make all kinds of noises
They spew out nothing but poison
To intimidate, they surround, surround, surround
And, oh, they think they are winning
And they're all boasting
But we've gone underground

You can't stop God's plan from happening
You can't stop the world from panicking
"The truth will set you free," oh
You can't stop His angels from ravaging
You can't stop this world from vanishing
"The truth will set you free," oh

You can't stop my God
You can't stop my God
You can't stop my God
No, you can't stop my God

Oh, I know we're feeling frightened
But whoever endures 'til the end   Matt 10:22
They will be saved
That's good enough for me

The World Is Burning

The world is burning, and I don't like the violence 2 Tim 3:1–5
And what was once wrong is now right Isa 5:20
Decent folks are silent
Our world gets darker
Evil grows stronger in the end and despite 2 Tim 3:13

The fifth seal's torn and the eleventh hour's at hand Rev 6:9–11
The birth pains are occurring closer Matt 24:1–14
Angels await for the command
But they are held back
Until there's more believers won over Matt 24:22

We are fighting a spiritual war Eph 6:12
So put on the full armor of God Eph 6:11
And stand your ground strong against the enemy
Our souls are free 1 Cor 9:1–2

These false prophets and these false teachers Matt 24:24
All these signs are pointing to His return
The angels' demeanor
Changes rapidly
Prepares for war
To put His glory front and center, center

We are fighting a spiritual war
So put on the full armor of God
And stand your ground strong against the enemy
Our souls are free
Our souls are free

Oh why? Oh why? Oh why?

We are fighting a spiritual war
So put on the full armor of God
And stand your ground strong against the enemy
Our souls are free

We are fighting a spiritual war
So put on the full armor of God
And stand your ground strong against the enemy
Our souls are free

We are fighting a spiritual war
So put on the full armor of God
And stand your ground strong against the enemy
Our souls are free
Our souls are free
Our souls are free

Be Prepared

*(Adapted from the melody of "Here Comes the Rain Again"
by Eurythmics)*

Sitting in my chair with my Bible
I come across numerous prophecies
Predicting all kinds of cultural erosion   2 Tim 3:2

Thinking of some actions to rescind
Forget all that you thought you knew
Both of these are interwoven
As I ponder in deep review

Consider thoughtfully what might be true
Cautiously what might ensue
Plausibly, a future preview

A warm light from the windowpane
The Book of Revelation describes so tragically
The Last Judgment coming as a fire explosion   Matt 13:40

A cloud causes the light to dim
You'd act differently if only you knew
What's coming your way in slow motion
What's your plan to get through?

Some thoughts are wrongfully
Misguided, askew
Horizontally
Your point of view
And not vertically as such they should   Ps 40:5

God's plan is flawlessly developing into
Don't let your faith wane   2 Tim 2:7–8

The final day will come just when
God decides it's time; gripping your rosary
Dealing with the scary, unexpected commotion
Can you please explain? Can you please explain?

Those who have disbelief, the greatest sin John 8:24
The Great Tribulation they must go through Rev 2:22
One last chance for heaven to reopen
Now do you believe? Renew?

Not for the brethren
Only for those who take the sign, amen Rev 14:9–11
The seven seals, trumpets, and bowls trajectory Rev 8:1–6
Being constantly pounded like a locomotion

Woe to those who don't find a Savior in Him
Only one outcome—you'll be excluded
Whether by implosion or explosion
Who else is there to turn to?

Don't you know that God's within? 1 Cor 3:16
Deep down inside, He's exemplary
Loving you with ever so much devotion?

And all you have to do is say "Yes!"

Kids These Days

There'll be times of difficulty coming in the last days   2 Tim 3:1–5
Kids are more concerned about their selfies that define
    their youth   2 Tim 3:2
When someone falls under attack, in the street they lay
They'd rather videotape and post the dispute

Now, lovers of self and of their pleasures
The Bible clearly warns to avoid this kind
Just turn your TV on to witness all the decay
Turning their backs on God and smirk while they disobey
Man, the times we're living in today

Those with good intentions are so few
They appear to be so reckless in what they do
They appear to be so heartless
They appear to be slanderous
They appear to be ungrateful; they appear swollen with conceit

When I take my time to investigate
No self-control evidenced by their remarks
Not me, instead I would proclaim His name   Rom 10:9–11
But You always knew they would depart

You knew of their rebellion when time began   Luke 16:15
Soon, they will indeed be justly God-damned
Are You slow to anger? Apropos.   Ps 86:15
But soon they'll find out. Welcome to Sheol!   Job 3:17
How shall Your grace be repaid?

Those with good intentions are so few
They appear to be so reckless in what they do
They appear to be so heartless
They appear to be slanderous
They appear to be ungrateful; they appear swollen with conceit

Those with good intentions are so few
They appear to be so reckless in what they do
They appear to be so heartless
They appear to be slanderous
They appear to be ungrateful; they appear swollen with conceit

Birth Pangs

(Adapted from the melody of "Hollywood's Bleeding"
by Post Malone)

Many are deceiving, safety's fleeting	Matt 24:11
Public judgments rushed	
Silenced voices, history's repeating	
Our neighbors swear distrust	

The media's misleading, and real victims pleading	
The same thing happened to Rome	
Selfishness practiced, sinfulness exceeding	Jas 3:16
Soon Jesus will take His throne	Matt 19:28

The time is almost here approaching quickly	Matt 24:3
Going to be your last chance to make known your vow	
You have to humble yourself and do it sincerely	2 Chr 34:27
Become aware of the truth and you must kneel down	Ps 95:6
You're nearly running out of time; this is not a joke	
The secret is believing and not being "woke"	Mark 16:16

Everywhere you look there's decay	
City up in flames, "all you can carry" buffet	
No police, liberal policies masqueraded	
Death and destruction in your face displayed	2 Tim 3:1–5

Just like animals, our society degrades	
Once the rapture happens, then only they'll remain	
Sent to the wilderness to wander	Ps 107:4
To reconsider their dishonor and ponder	

Where they turned away from Thee	Isa 59:13
Three and a half years left to agree	Dan 12:7
Final judgment guaranteed	Rom 2:5
The Lake of Fire is His decree	Rev 21:8

Pestilence, no travel	Luke 21:11
This is substantial	
Just wake up, hello; there's a roaming foe	1 Pet 5:8
We see examples on TV channels	
Hidden demons from down below	1 John 4:1–3

The time is almost here approaching quickly
Going to be your last chance to make known your vow
You have to humble yourself and do it sincerely
Become aware of the truth and you must kneel down
You're nearly running out of time; this is not a joke
The secret is believing and not being "woke"

With A Crown

*(Adapted from the melody of "What Goes Around . . .
Comes Around" by Justin Timberlake)*

Look around, do you think our God has a plan?   Acts 2:23
Are you shocked by what's observed?
He's been aware since time began   Isa 46:10

So much chaos on display
Pleasure on demand in your hand
Life seems to be in decay   2 Tim 3:1–5
Selfishness abounds but His grace has prolonged   Rom 2:4

No one will submit, way too much conflict
We're all hypocrites; soon, there'll be no more delay
We're all so unfit, need someone to remit
Who can acquit? Deliver us from despair   Rom 10:9–10

Awareness will come with the breakdown
There's only so much you can deny
When right is wrong and wrong is right is espoused   Isa 5:20–21
And pointless questions like "Why?"

There's a building pressure that surrounds us
Only a few are aware of what this implies
The end's approaching; it's all by His design

With a sound, with a sound, with a sound   Rev 8:1–13
His return will astound
With a frown, with a frown, with a frown
Unbelievers will countdown
On the ground, on the ground, on the ground   Rev 16:16
There's gonna be a showdown
And with a crown, with a crown, with a crown   Rev 19:12–16
He's gonna be renowned, yeah

Fortunately, there is a Savior who's been named
Appointed by God Himself
Soon, He'll be proclaimed   Mark 8:27–33
The Scriptures will be fulfilled   Matt 5:17–18
He freely received all our blame   1 Cor 15:3–8
Don't be dismayed
Heaven: there's a way to claim, and you can belong

No one will submit, way too much conflict
We're all hypocrites; soon, there'll be no more delay
We're all so unfit, need someone to remit
Who can acquit? Deliver us from despair

Awareness will come with the breakdown
There's only so much you can deny
When right is wrong and wrong is right is espoused
And pointless questions like "Why?"

There's a building pressure that surrounds us
Only a few are aware of what this implies
The end's approaching; it's all by His design

With a sound, with a sound, with a sound
His return will astound
With a frown, with a frown, with a frown
Unbelievers will countdown
On the ground, on the ground, on the ground
There's gonna be a showdown
And with a crown, with a crown, with a crown
He's gonna be renowned, yeah

And with a sound and some frowns—on the ground, He'll be crowned
And with a sound and some frowns—on the ground, He'll be crowned
And with a sound and some frowns—on the ground, He'll be crowned
And with a sound and some frowns—on the ground, He'll be crowned

No one will submit, way too much conflict
We're all hypocrites; soon, there'll be no more delay
We're all so unfit, need someone to remit
Who can acquit? Deliver us from despair

Awareness will come with the breakdown
There's only so much you can deny
When right is wrong and wrong is right is espoused
And pointless questions like "Why?"

There's a building pressure that surrounds us
Only a few are aware of what this implies
The end's approaching; it's all by His design

With a sound, with a sound, with a sound
His return will astound
With a frown, with a frown, with a frown
Unbelievers will countdown
On the ground, on the ground, on the ground
There's gonna be a showdown
And with a crown, with a crown, with a crown
He's gonna be renowned, yeah

Let me explain this the way I see it:
You don't wanna be unknown or be on your own   Eph 2:12–13
To be secluded and you not to have Him atone   1 John 2:2
Don't be without
Life's too short, there's no guarantees
You don't wanna be disowned

He's returning to this world   Matt 24:36
Escaping is absurd
Change your ways now or forever you could burn
All of this has been foretold
Believe in Jesus Christ and His righteousness is
     conferred   Rom 10:9–11

You can change today, don't wait for your last rites
Do this so that with God your soul and spirit reunite
He created you; And He loves you so unconditionally   Jer 1:5

And with a sound, He will be crowned
Do you wanna be exposed?
And with a sound, He will be crowned
Do you wanna be disposed of?
And with a sound, He will be crowned
Or do you wanna be consoled?
And with a sound, He will be crowned
Or do you wanna be remolded?

Surrender to Him (Hey, hey, hey, hey, hey, hey, hey)   Luke 9:23–24
Surrender to Him (Hey, hey, hey, hey, hey, hey, hey)

Has any of this made sense maybe?
Surrender to Him (Hey, hey, hey, hey, hey, hey, hey, hey, hey)
Surrender to Him (Hey, hey, hey, hey, hey)

And with a sound, He will be crowned

Revelation Timeline

(Adapted from the melody of "Man in the Mirror"
by Michael Jackson)

This message may sound strange, but the end has arrived   Matt 24
Some are left to endure, others raptured and gone   1 Thess 4:17
Try to use this guide

Once the Church Age ends and the Great Tribulation
    begins   Matt 24:21
Many will be left behind
His timeline's nearly complete; one more chance to flee
Don't find yourself blind to everything you're about to reside

Fires in the backdrop, there's nothing that can stop   2 Pet 3
His judgment will be poured out   Ezek 7:8
This is the beginning of several sorrows
Many will have wished to forego
Today, not tomorrow

It's so true that the LORD should be feared   Deut 6:13
Time's running out in these final days
Instead, God should have been more revered
You have to speak with your mouth to be ordained   Rom 10:9
Jesus has to be your Savior for this exchange

The scrolls have been unrolled; the outcome's been
    foretold   Rev 5:1
Many will be penalized
They ignored what was known, now exist alone
Many have made the choice not to believe and instead have
    roamed   Exod 16:3

Forever, you'll be apart; your ego's falsely smart
In Hell, no one will hear your screams
When the LORD returns, there'll be no more pleas; only judgment
    and no mercy
Sadly, this is what's guaranteed

It's so true that the LORD should be feared
Time's running out in these final days
Instead, God should have been more revered
You have to speak with your mouth to be ordained
Jesus has to be your Savior for this exchange

It's so true that the LORD should be feared
Time's running out in these final days
Instead, God should have been more revered
You have to speak with your mouth to be ordained
Jesus has to be your Savior for this EXCHANGE

It's so true that the LORD should be feared
Time's running out in these final days
Instead, God should have been more revered
You have to speak with your mouth to be ordained
Jesus has to be your Savior for this exchange
God lets you decide because He's so kind
So don't be fooled, don't be surprised

The LORD, the LORD, the LORD
The LORD, the LORD, the LORD

Hello?
You have to speak with your mouth to be ordained
Jesus has to be your Savior for this EXCHANGE
Is this understood?
This message may sound strange
Some are left to endure
Message—strange
Can't save yourself

Hello?
You've got to adopt this yourself
This message may sound strange—today
The LORD should be feared
You want to, you want to discover Your Father

Hello?
This may sound strange
Indeed, this is God's plan—His plan
You want to, you want to approve of God's Son, God's Son
You want to—hands up, hands up, this may sound strange
Hands up
Hands up and resist yourself, now
The LORD should be feared
This message may sound strange
The LORD should be feared
Now show it, now show it, now show it

Hello?
Strange, this may be strange

Spiritual Battleground

(Adapted from the melody of "Safe and Sound" by Capital Cities)

Jesus drank our cup; He bore God's curse on that tree   Gal 3:13
He received every sin for me   Heb 7:27

He cared to instruct
Shortly, there'll be a showdown
Soon, a spiritual battleground, spiritual battleground   Eph 6:12

It's time for us to stand up, acknowledge what contaminates
Soon, He'll eradicate

Excellent conduct; don't just fall in line with the crowd
Don't be afraid to speak out loud

Spiritual battleground, spiritual battleground
The mighty will be confounded
Spiritual battleground   1 Cor 1:27–31

He'll return from above; in like manner, His journey   Acts 1:11
To bring peace and victory

We cannot be plucked; there's no need to fool
     around   John 10:27–29
God's grace will superabound, spiritual battleground   Rom 5:20

Spiritual battleground, spiritual battleground
The mighty will be confounded, spiritual battleground

It'll be abrupt; mournful, the wicked will flee   Rev 3:3
He will blatantly ignore their pleas

They'll be awestruck; shortly after the trumpet's
    sound   Ezek 33:3–5
Soon, a spiritual battleground

For those who are corrupt; His final judgment delivered concisely
The Lake of Fire precisely   Rev 20:15

Please put all your trust: in Jesus who was mocked
    with a crown   Matt 27:27–29
Soon, a spiritual battleground

Spiritual battleground, spiritual battleground, spiritual battleground,
    spiritual battleground
Spiritual battleground, spiritual battleground
The mighty will be confounded, spiritual battleground

The Return

(Adapted from the melody of "Rushing Back" by Flume, feat. Vera Blue)

Some people live their lives oblivious and soon they will be surprised
It'll be their own fault that they ignored His calls causing their
    demise   John 3:36

There's still some time left to devote yourself and get all your affairs
    aligned
But if you instead decide to decline then indeed hell will be assigned

Jesus Christ is coming back, coming back   Matt 24:44
Jesus Christ is coming back, coming back
Jesus Christ is coming back, coming back
Jesus Christ is coming back, coming back
You can't live today in the flesh and just simply ignore
He gave you free will but there surely will be consequences in store

I'm sharing this warning: I beg you to reconsider, this I implore
There'll come a time when you'll have to choose exactly what you
    stand for

Jesus Christ is coming back, coming back
Jesus Christ is coming back, coming back
Jesus Christ is coming back, coming back
Jesus Christ is coming back, coming back

Old things have passed away, you're a new creature who's brand
    new   2 Cor 5:17
In an instant quite abrupt; you're redeemed and rightfully just
                                          1 Thess 4:17

And once you believe, live out your faith and consider getting
    baptized   Rom 10:9
Your heart will heal up and your soul will be saved and intimately
    intertwined

You'll cherish those who led you to Christ; all these memories
    will remind
Grateful for their persistent efforts to guide the Holy Spirit
    to reside   Matt 13:1–23

Jesus Christ is coming back, coming back
Jesus Christ is coming back, coming back
Jesus Christ is coming back, coming back
Jesus Christ is coming back
And He'll stay

Jesus Christ is coming back, coming back
Jesus Christ is coming back, coming back
Jesus Christ is coming back, coming back
Jesus Christ is coming back, coming back

About the Author

Eric Zack is a born-again Christian who resorted to poetry as his preferred emotional outlet at the age of twenty years old. At that time, his dear mother died from metastatic cancer at the age of thirty-nine years old. His mother's cancer was not directly talked about in the open with him or his three younger brothers, although she was diagnosed several years before her death. He was raised in a stable middle-class home environment in a small town in the middle of the United States in the Roman Catholic faith and served as an altar boy for several years growing up. He had a difficult time processing what had happened and stepped away from his faith temporarily as he coped and adjusted with this "new normal." Fortunately, he soon returned to his faith with a renewed passion to develop a closer relationship with his Savior Jesus Christ while trying to better understand life, suffering, loss, and healing. His personal mission statement and professional goals have been to "make a difference and help others" because he was not able to do so for his mother.

Since a young age, Eric has generally possessed an introvert personality type and has often kept his thoughts and feelings private for the most part until now. He is also an experienced and expert oncology nurse and nursing college professor in response to his mom's death, which occurred during his third year of college. Today, he is married and has four adult children, none of whom has ever met his mother. Eric's poetry has dealt with most aspects of living life and covers many different, unique topics that most human beings will experience. More recently, he has been driven to write about many aspects of his maturing Christian faith. He noted a significant gap in the literature in regard to Christian poetry that is supported by the Holy Bible and the many truths that the Holy Bible shares. As a result, he wanted to publish his poetry collections to share with whomever is interested in learning more about these topics, whomever enjoys reading and meditating on various Bible verses, and whomever enjoys poetry in general. He felt it a priority at this time in his life to pursue publishing these five volumes to help others in their spiritual journeys given today's serious crises and waning timeline.

His other poetry collections that are not directly related to Christianity may be published at a future date. Eric's poetry style is typically rhythmic and rhyming in nature with repeated chorus lines (almost like a song) to support certain important aspects worth stressing. Up to this point, his poems have been hidden from all and considered amateur (never shared or published before). This has been his "quiet" passion for over thirty years now; and he hopes that some good may come out of him sharing these authentic, cherished poems that are very personal and private in nature. He sincerely believes that the Holy Spirit has coauthored most of these, using him as a vessel to reach others who are in desperate need of answers and/or support.

Thank you for allowing small pieces of me and my life's insight into your reality and life. And may Jesus Christ have all the power, praise, and glory for doing so. And may God continue to bless you and your loved ones as you seek to get closer and closer to Him. In Christ Jesus, Eric.